Essential Scales for

Electric Bass

Major Scale Modes and Pentatonic Scales

by **Max Palermo**

Acknowledgments:

Special thanks for all of their support to Patrizia Sandrini, Aaron Stang, Nancy Rehm and everyone at Warner Bros. Publications and Haleh Kamyab.

Project Manager: **Aaron Stang**
Production Coordinator: **Karl Bork**
Art Design: **Carmen Fortunato**

WARNER BROS. PUBLICATIONS
Warner Music Group
An AOL Time Warner Company
USA: 15800 NW 48th Avenue, Miami, FL 33014

IMP
INTERNATIONAL MUSIC PUBLICATIONS LIMITED
ENGLAND: GRIFFIN HOUSE,
161 HAMMERSMITH ROAD, LONDON W6 8BS

Contents

*I*ntroduction

The aim of this publication is to provide students of all levels a simple and quick reference guide to a wide-ranging and complex subject: *the scales and their relative modes*.

In each chapter you will find an introductory chart explaining the structure and theory of the scale in question, as well as its practical application. The development of the scales in all the keys follows, together with the fingering and tablature for 4 and 5-string basses.

Acquainting yourself with using the scales is an important goal to reach. When used correctly, scales complement the harmonic structure of a piece of music and increase the choice of different sounds, enriching these sounds with new and diverse nuances.

I would therefore advise you to pause after each chapter, taking the time to absorb all the information contained within it. Repeat the scales with a metronome (or a drum machine) and then at the end try and make up your own riffs, both in isolation and as part of a bass line; always keeping the chords of reference in mind.

As these scales are used a lot in different types of music (jazz, fusion, funk, rock...) you will have at your disposal a personal repertoire of patterns that you can use in different harmonic progressions.

Enjoy your work!

The MAJOR SCALE Family

The Major Scale

Major scale (Ionian mode)

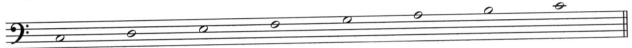

C Major (construction)

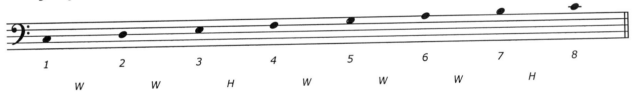

One octave scale

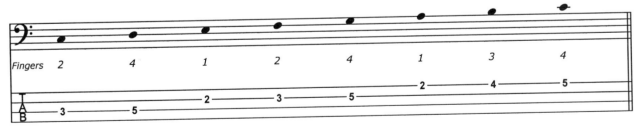

Chords

2 Octaves

C Major (Ionian)

D♭ Major

D Major

E♭ Major

2 Octaves

E Major

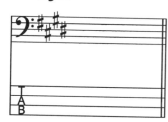

Ema⁷

F Major

Fma⁷

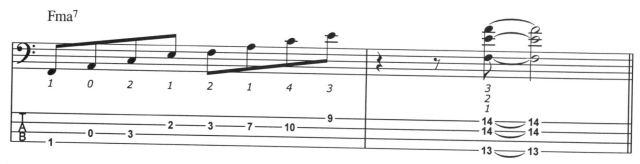

F# Major

F#ma7

G Major

Gma7

2 Octaves

Aᵇ Major

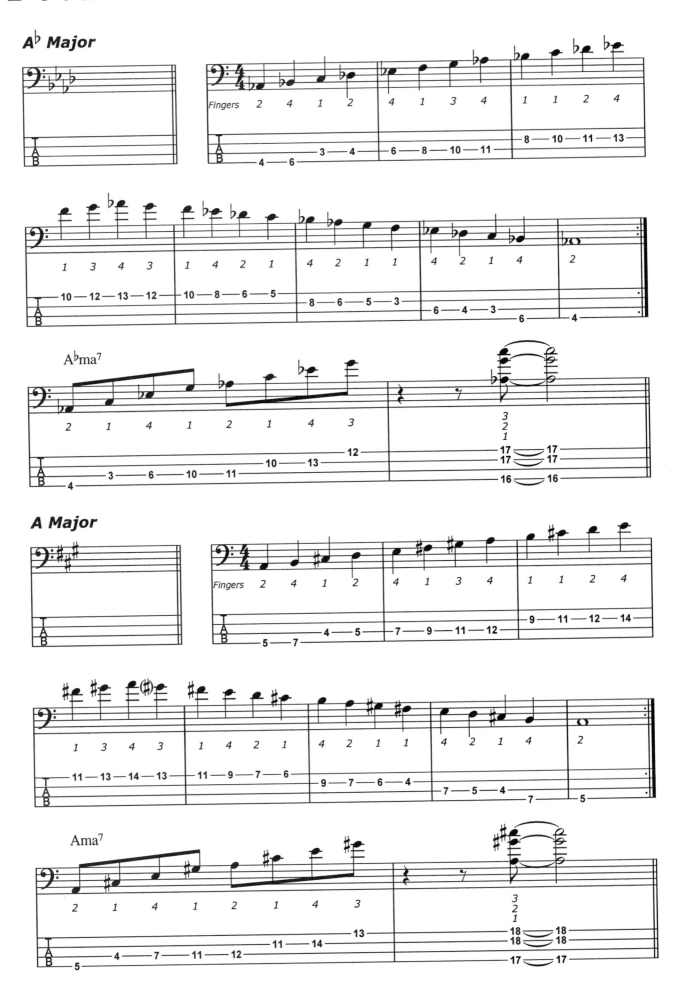

A Major

Major Scale

B♭ Major

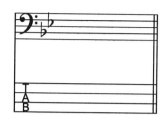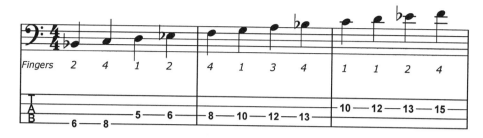

B Major

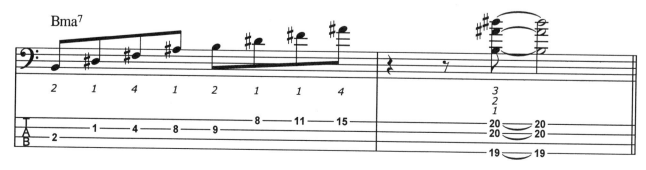

3 Octaves

B Major

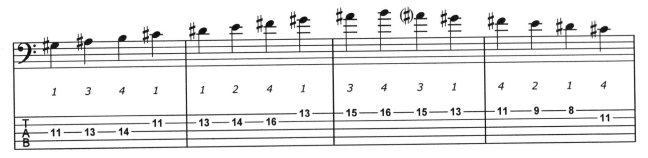

C Major

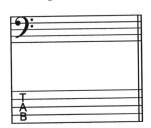
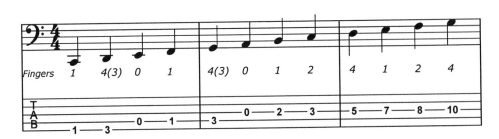

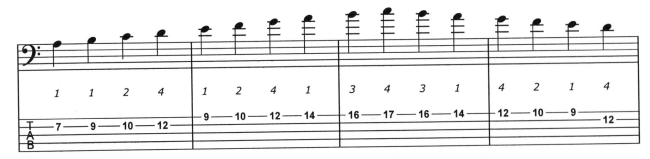

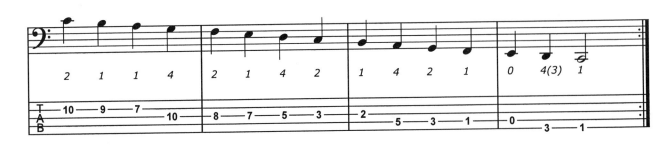

D Major

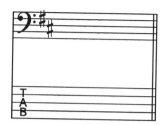

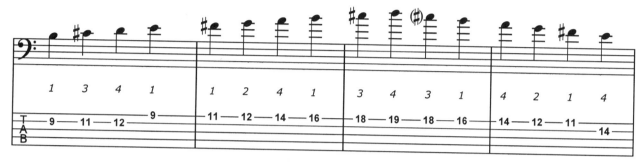

E Major

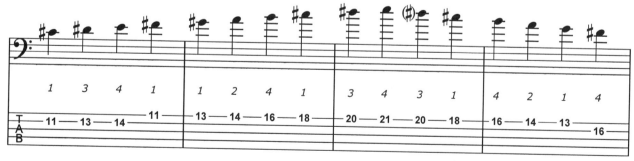

The Dorian Mode

Major scale

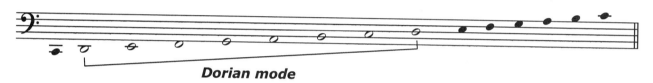

Dorian mode

C Dorian (construction)

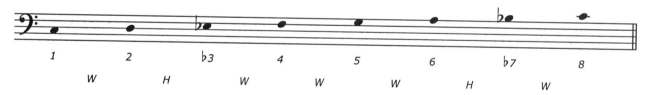

1	2	♭3	4	5	6	♭7	8
W	H	W	W	W	H	W	

One octave scale

Chords

Cm   Cm⁶   Cm⁶/⁹   Cm⁷   Cm⁹

2 Octaves

C Dorian

C# Dorian

Dorian Mode

D Dorian

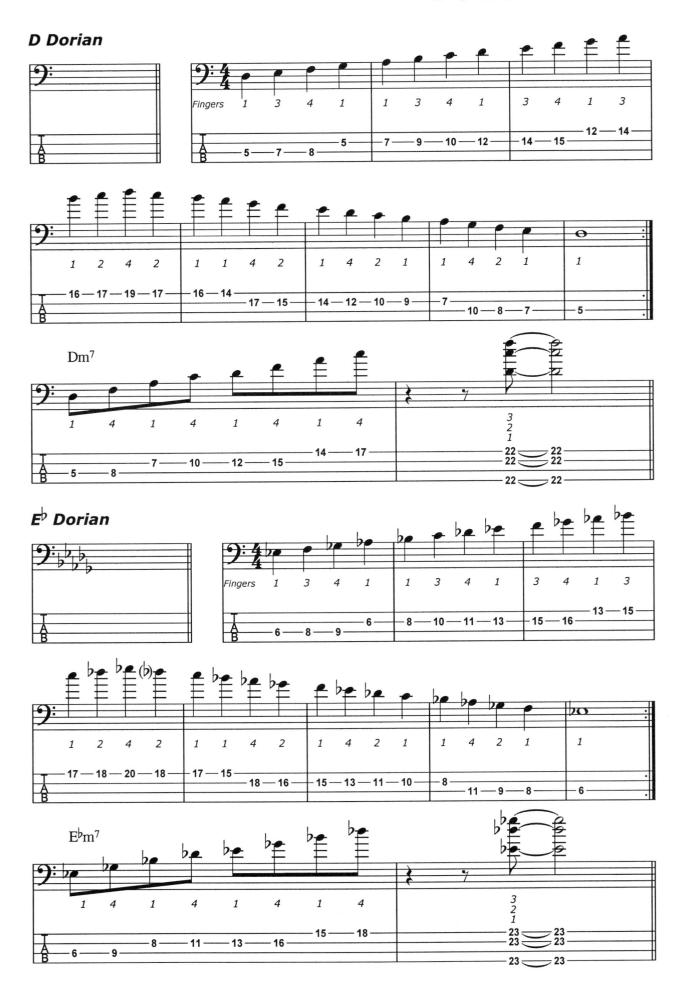

17

2 Octaves

E Dorian

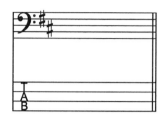

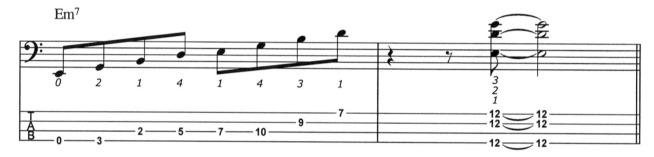

F Dorian

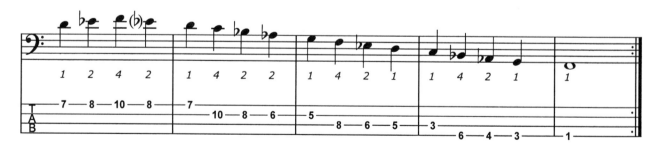

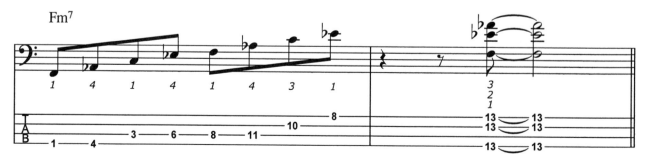

Dorian Mode

F# Dorian

G Dorian

19

2 Octaves

A♭ Dorian

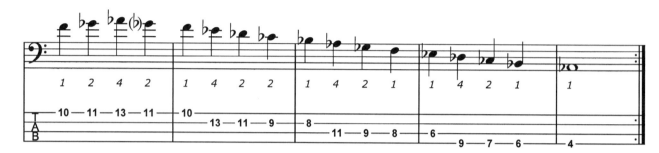

A♭m⁷

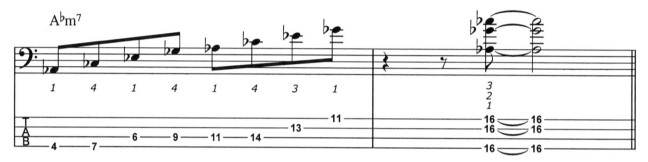

A Dorian

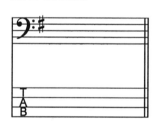

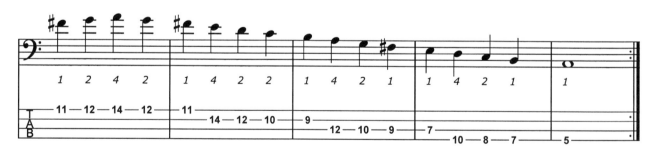

Am⁷

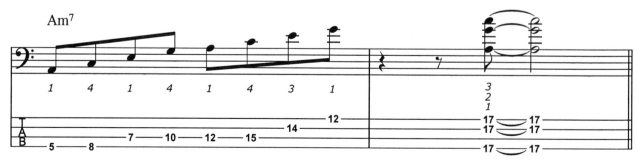

B♭ Dorian

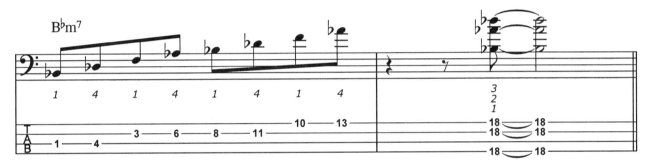

B Dorian

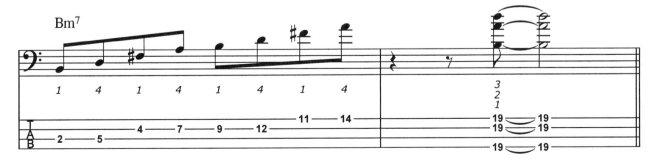

3 Octaves

B Dorian

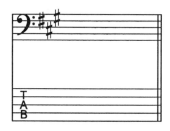

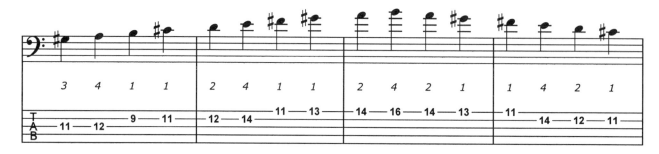

C Dorian

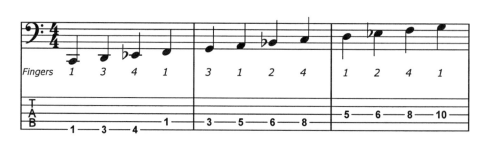

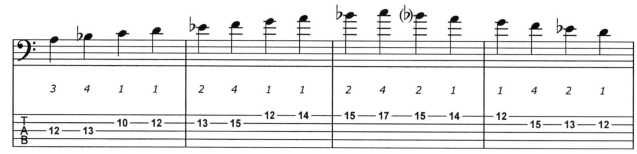

D Dorian

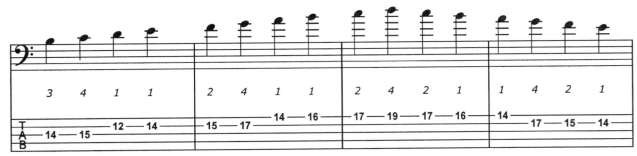

E Dorian

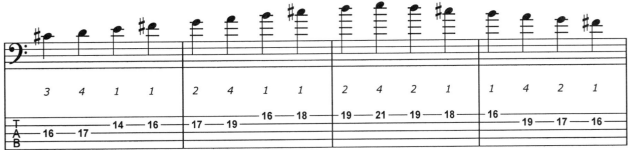

The Phrygian Mode

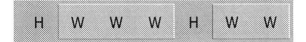

Major scale

Phrygian mode

C Phrygian (construction)

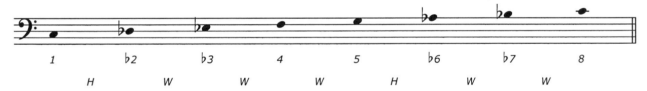

One octave scale

Chords

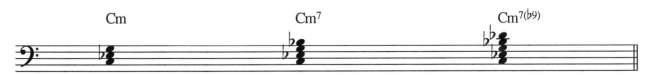

2 Octaves

C Phrygian

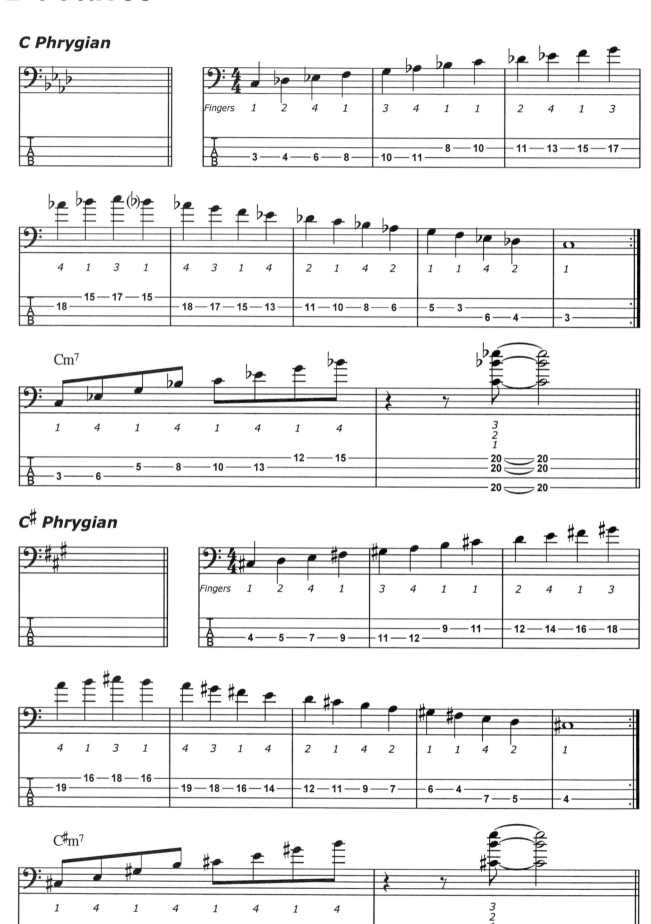

C# Phrygian

Phrygian Mode

D Phrygian

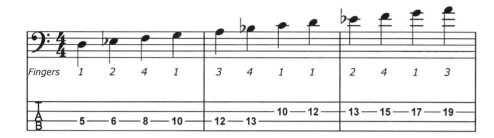

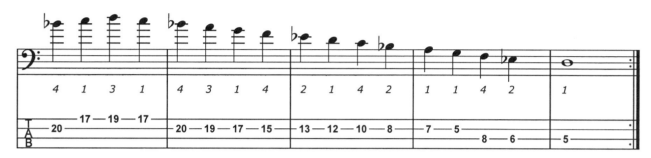

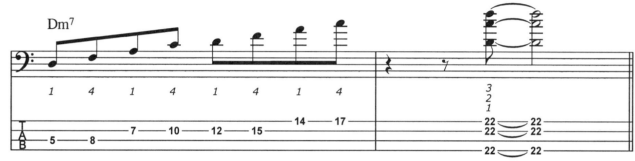

D♯ Phrygian

2 Octaves

E Phrygian

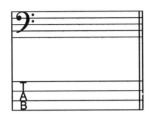

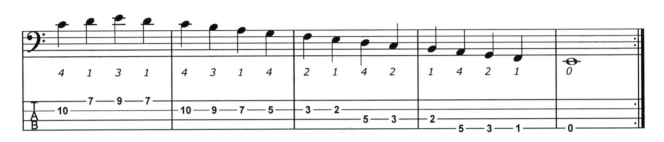

Em[7]

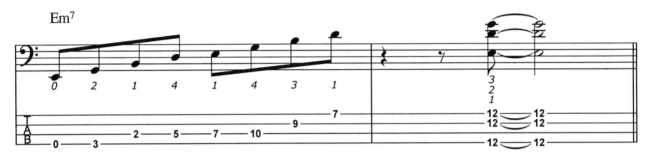

F Phrygian

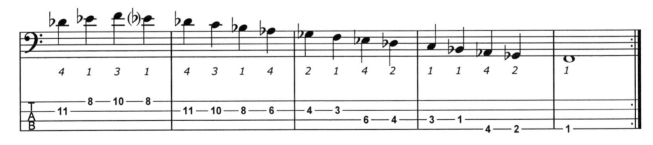

Fm[7]

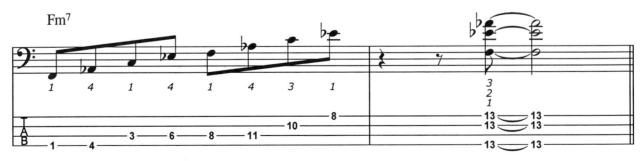

28

F# Phrygian

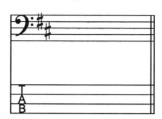

F#m7

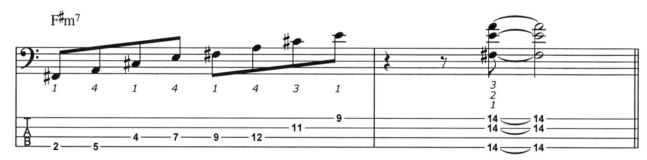

G Phrygian

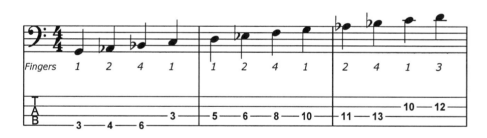

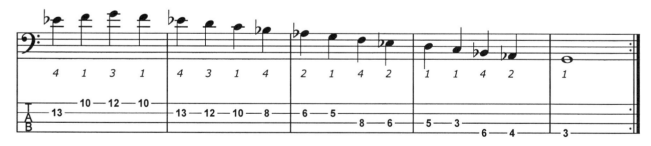

Gm7

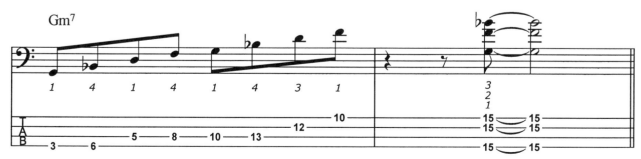

2 Octaves

G# Phrygian

A Phrygian

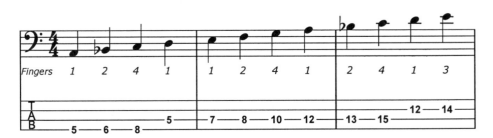

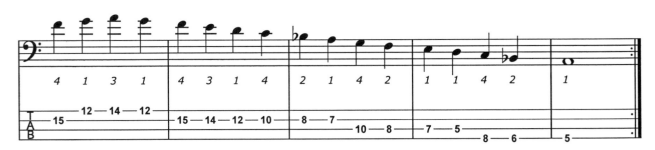

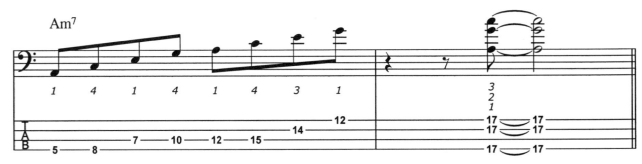

B♭ Phrygian

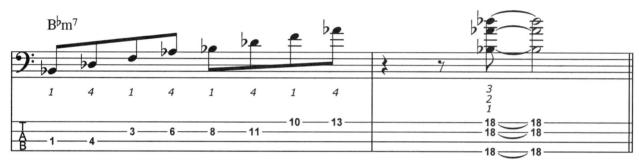

B Phrygian

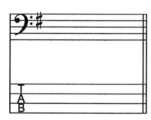

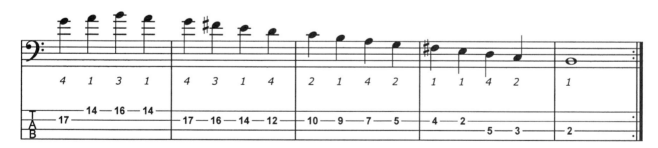

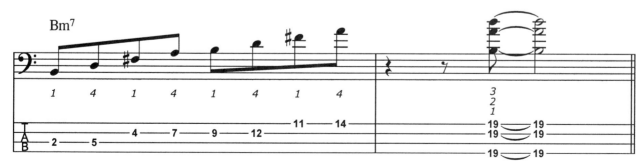

3 Octaves

B Phrygian

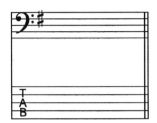

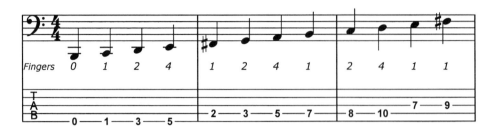

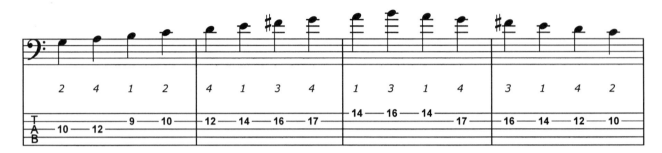

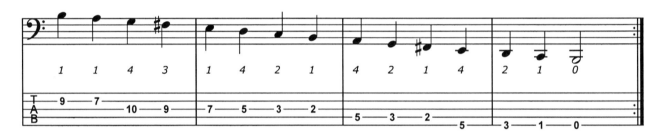

C Phrygian

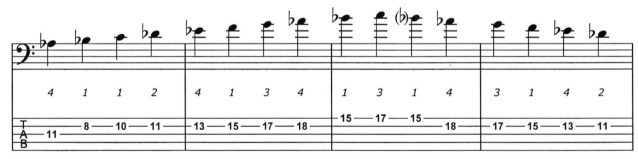

Phrygian Mode

D Phrygian

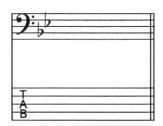

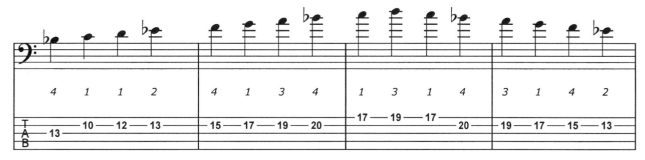

E Phrygian

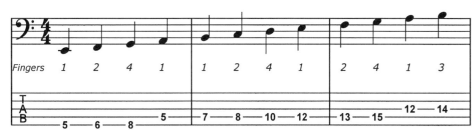

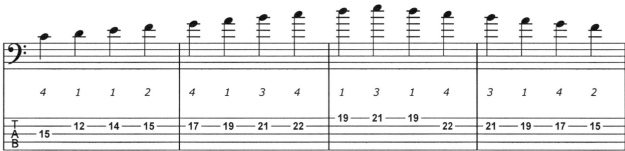

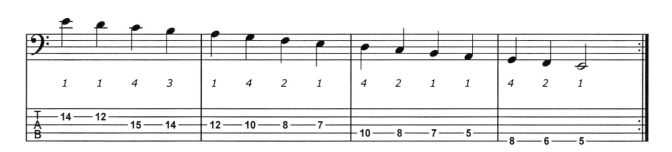

The Lydian Mode

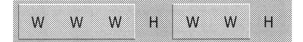

Major scale

Lydian mode

C Lydian (construction)

One octave scale

Chords

2 Octaves

C Lydian

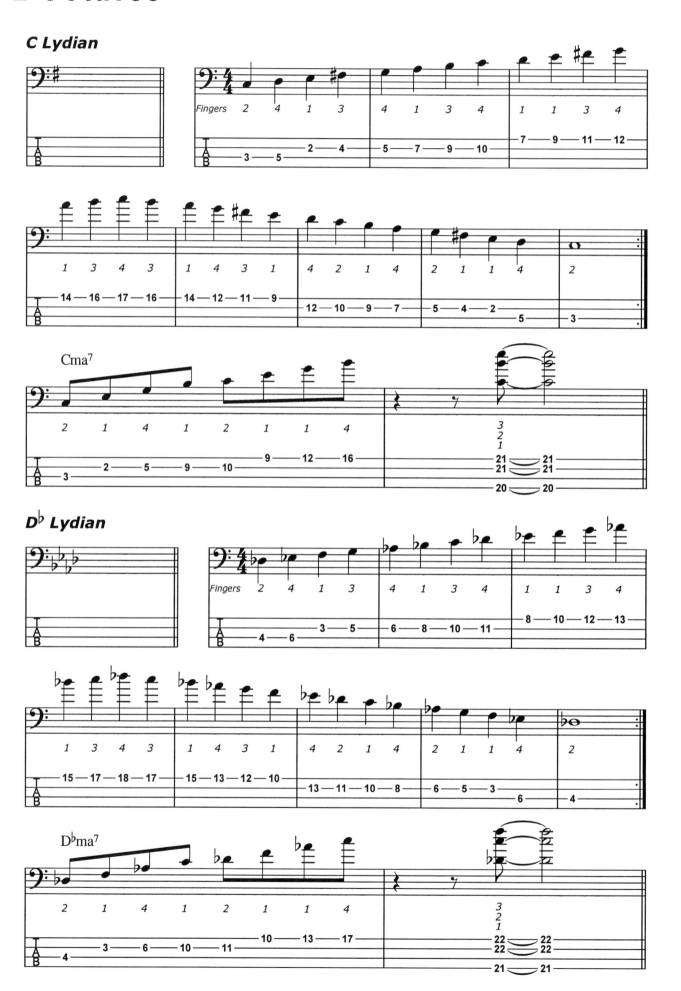

D♭ Lydian

36

Lydian Mode

D Lydian

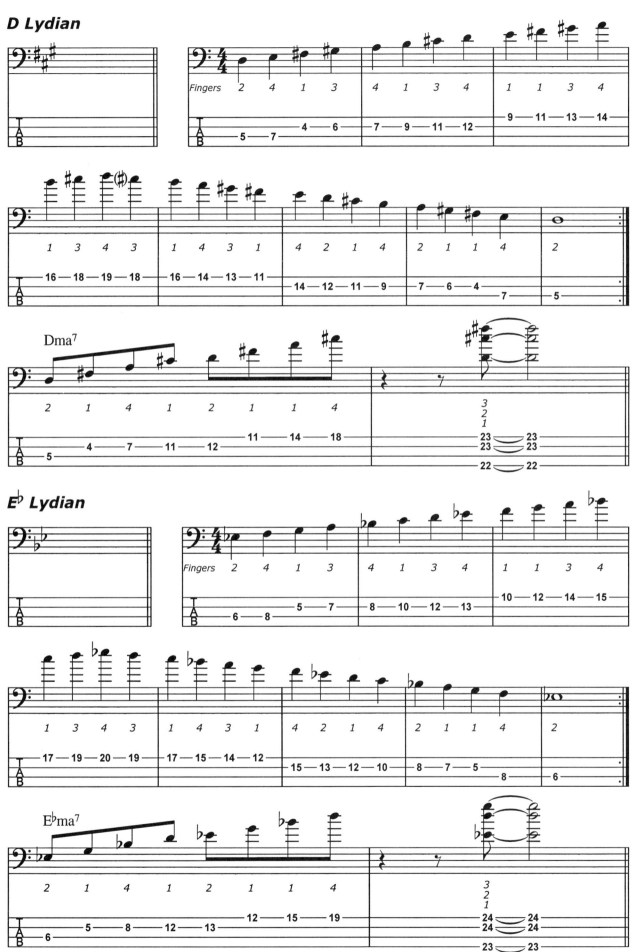

Eb Lydian

2 Octaves

E Lydian

Ema⁷

F Lydian

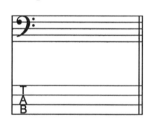

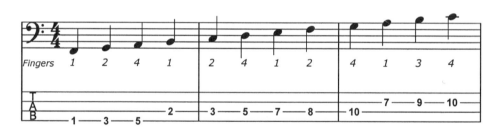

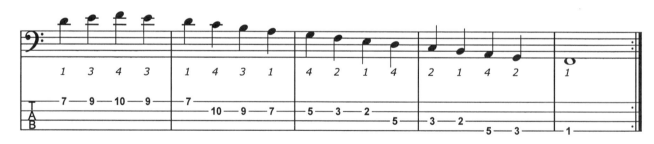

Fma⁷

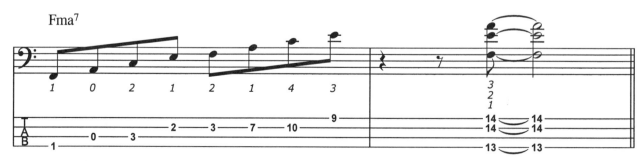

Lydian Mode

G♭ Lydian

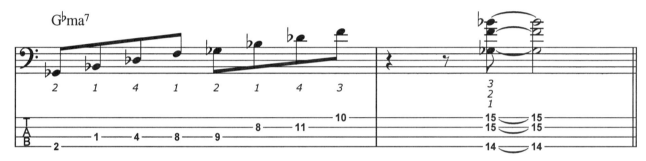

G♭ma7

G Lydian

Gma7

39

2 Octaves

A♭ Lydian

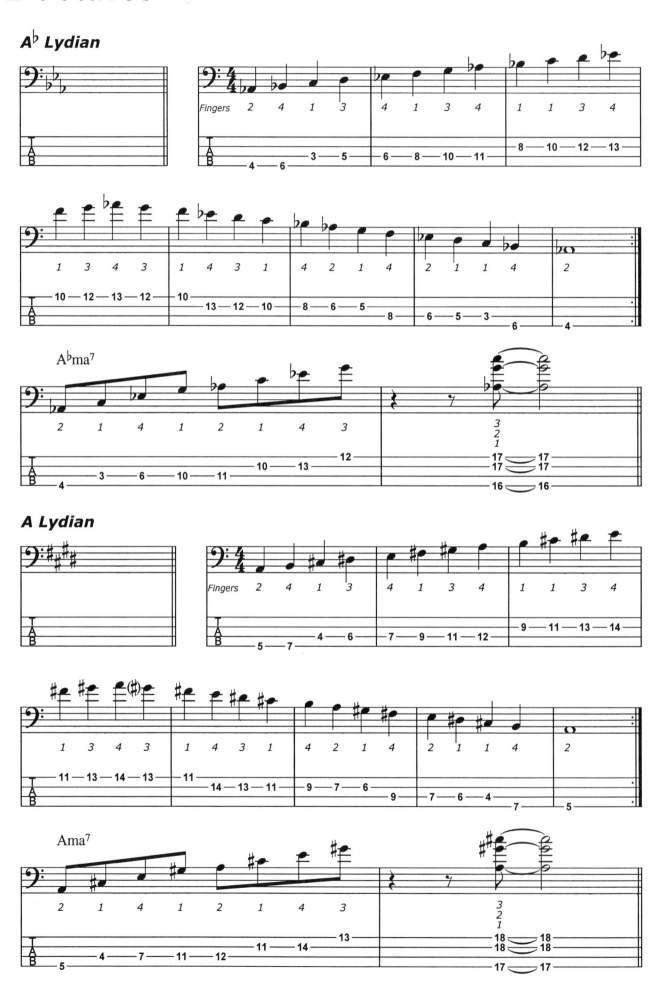

A♭ma⁷

A Lydian

Ama⁷

40

B♭ Lydian

B Lydian

3 Octaves

B Lydian

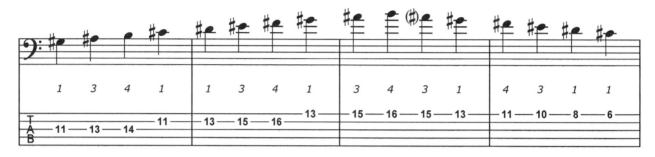

C Lydian

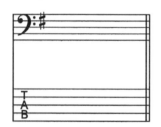

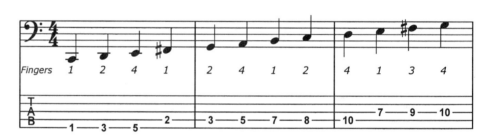

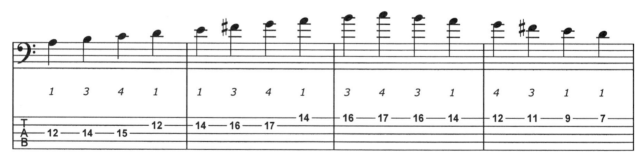

42

Lydian Mode

D Lydian

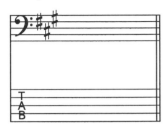

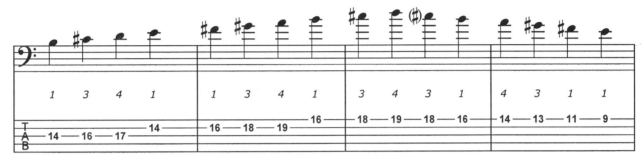

E Lydian

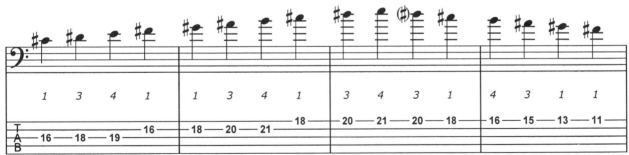

The Mixolydian Mode

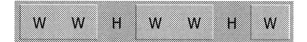

Major scale

Mixolydian mode

C Mixolydian (construction)

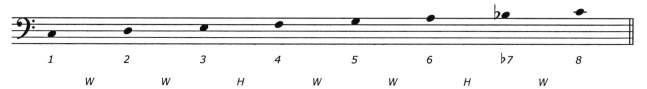

One octave scale

Chords

2 Octaves

C Mixolydian

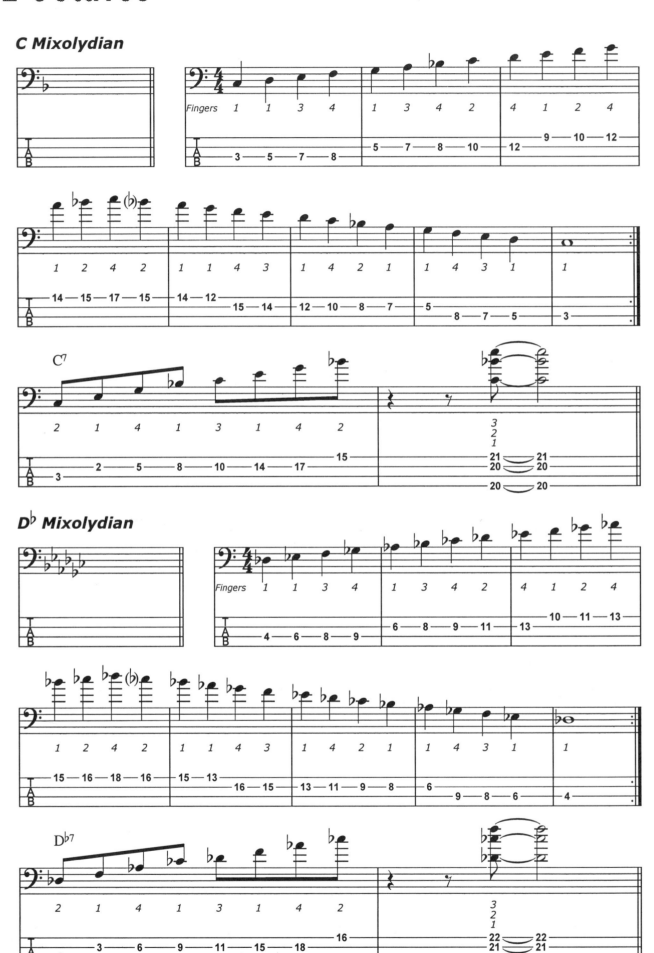

Db Mixolydian

D Mixolydian

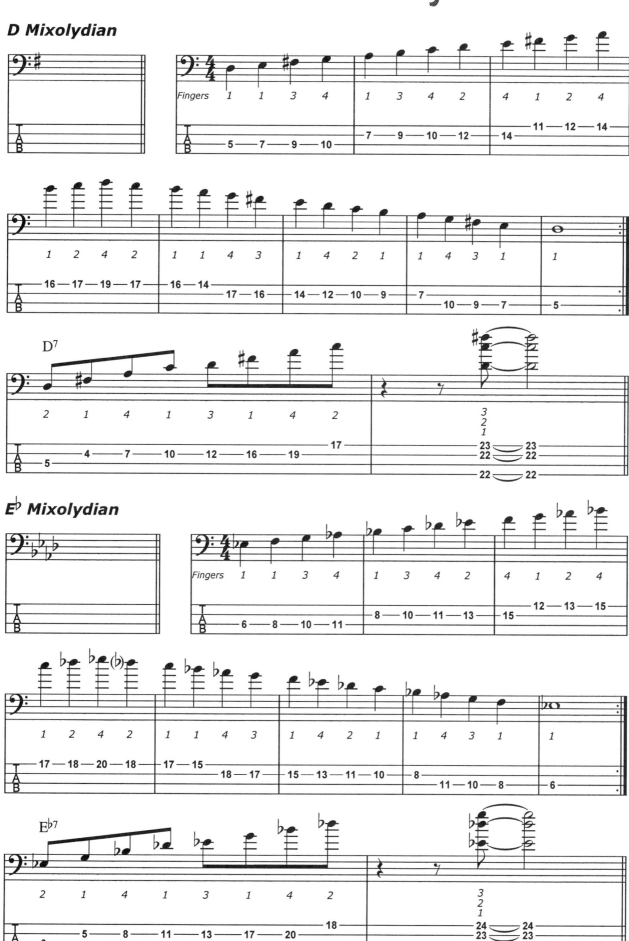

E♭ Mixolydian

2 Octaves

E Mixolydian

F Mixolydian

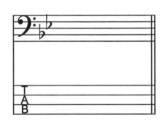

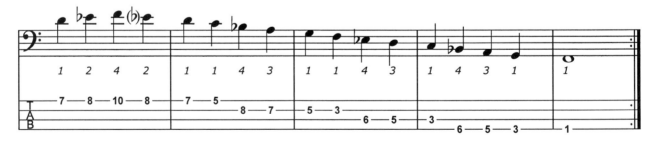

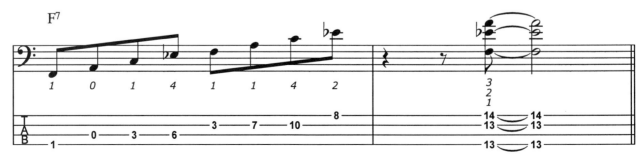

Mixolydian Mode

F# Mixolydian

G Mixolydian

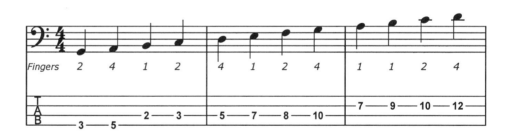

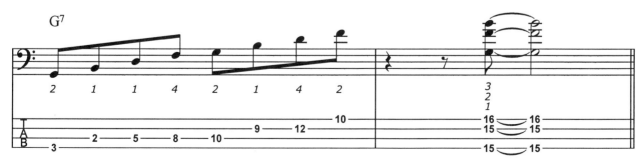

49

2 Octaves

A♭ Mixolydian

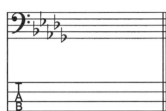

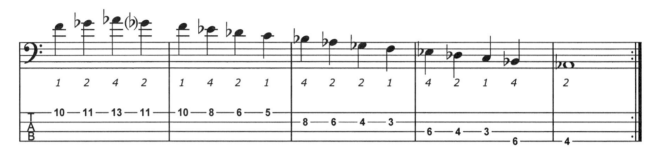

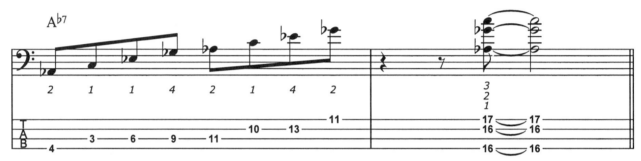

A Mixolydian

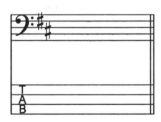
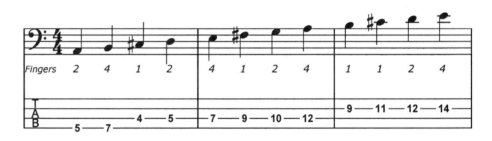

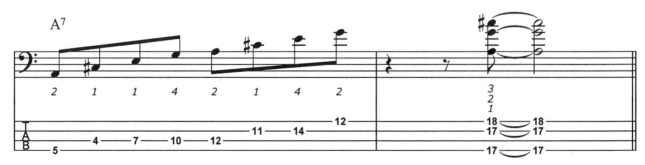

B♭ Mixolydian

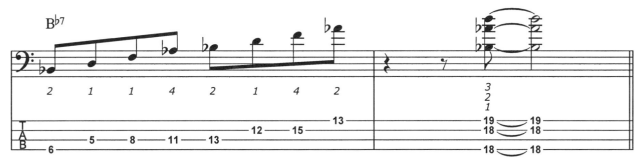

B Mixolydian

3 Octaves

B Mixolydian

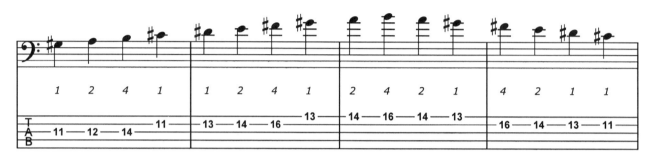

C Mixolydian

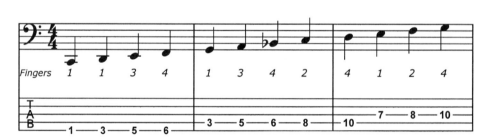

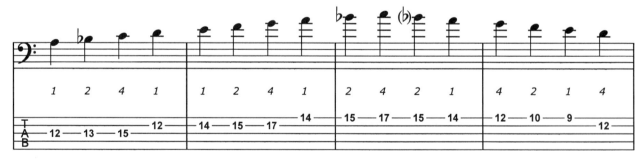

D Mixolydian

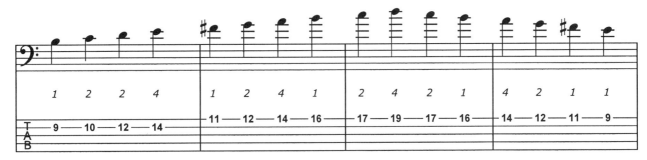

E Mixolydian

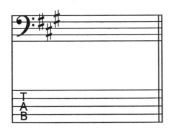
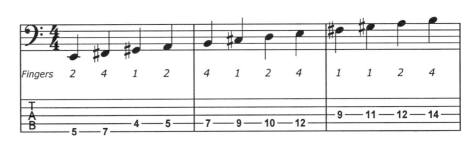

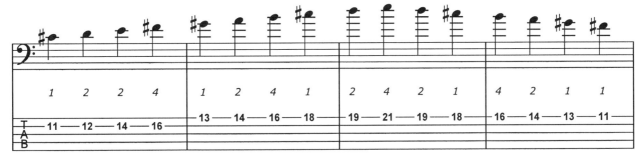

The Natural Minor Scale

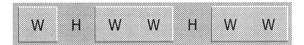

Major scale

Natural Minor scale (Aeolian mode)

C Minor (construction)

1	2	♭3	4	5	♭6	♭7	8
W	H	W	W	H	W	W	

One octave scale

Fingers   1   3   4   1   3   4   1   3

Chords

Cm   Cm^(♭6)   Cm^7   Cm^7(♭6)   Cm^9

2 Octaves

C Minor (Aeolian)

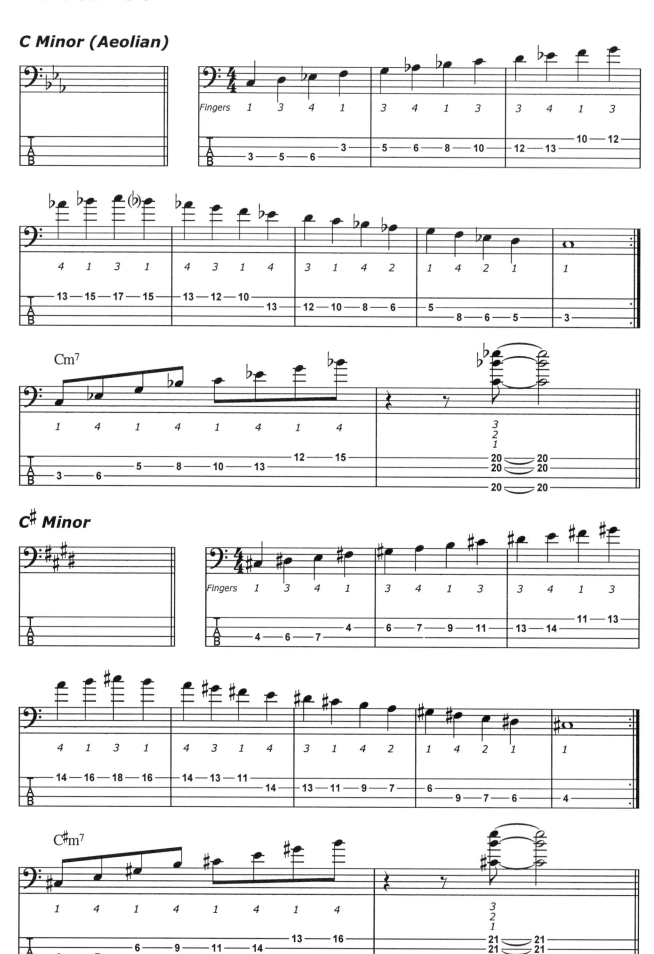

C# Minor

D Minor

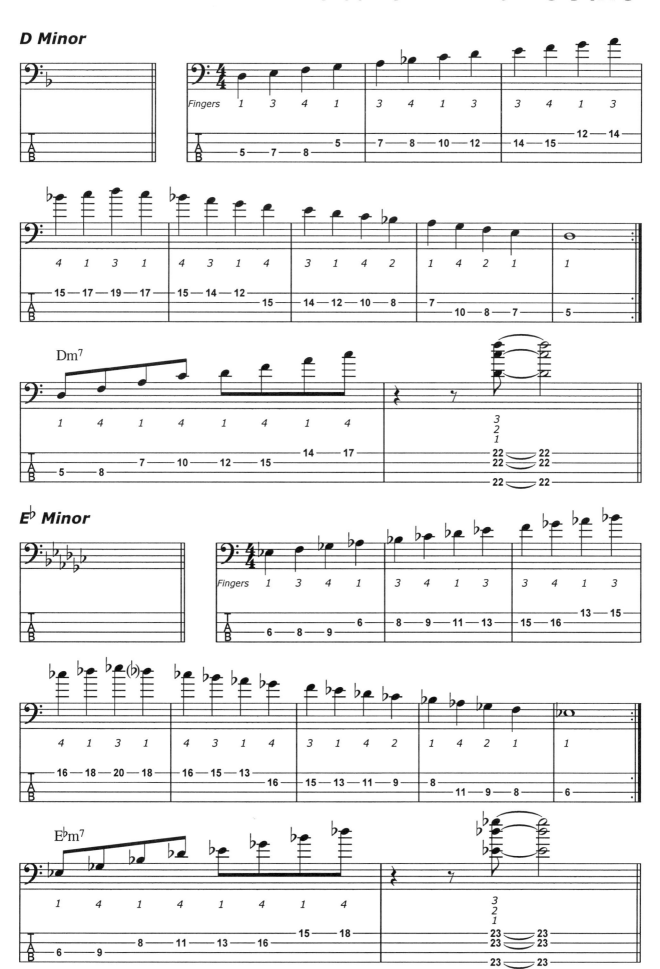

E♭ Minor

2 Octaves

E Minor

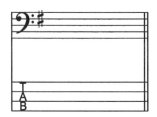 

Em⁷

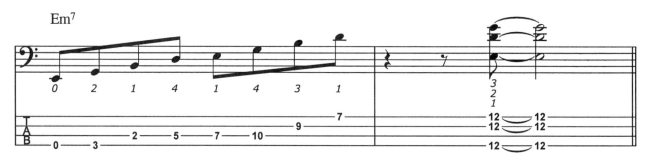

F Minor

Fm⁷

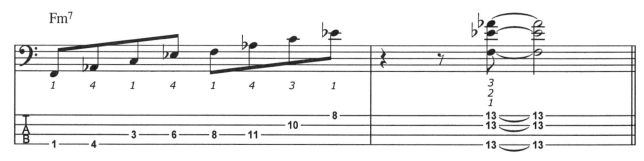

58

Natural Minor Scale

F# Minor

G Minor

2 Octaves

G# Minor

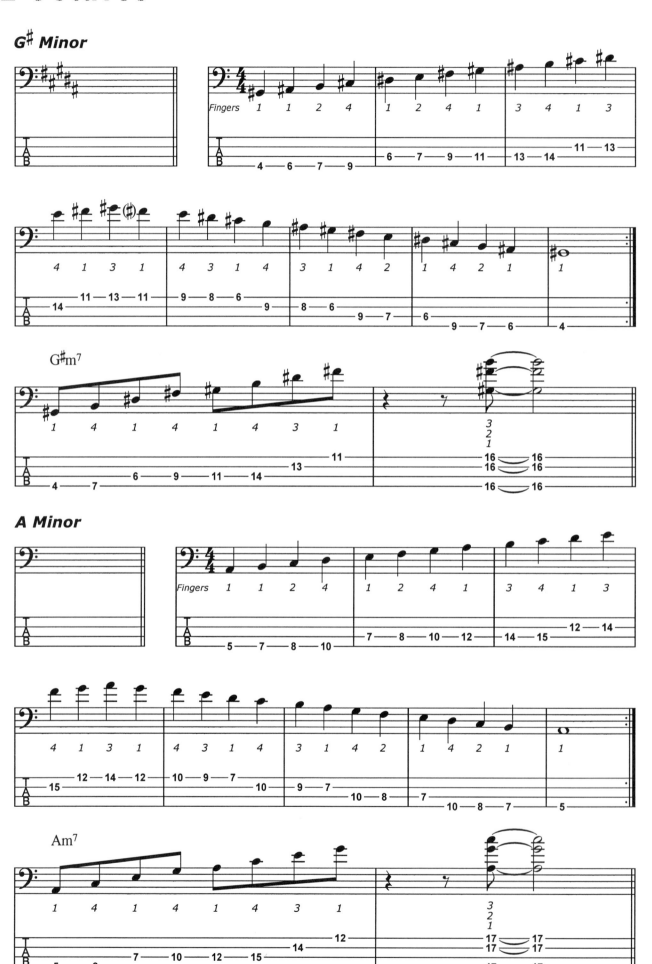

A Minor

3 Octaves

B Minor

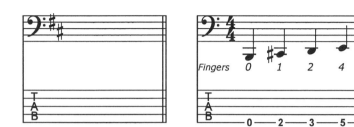

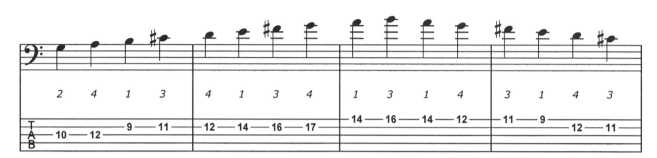

C Minor

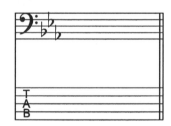

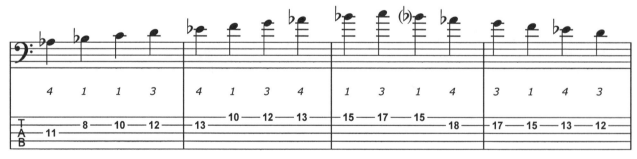

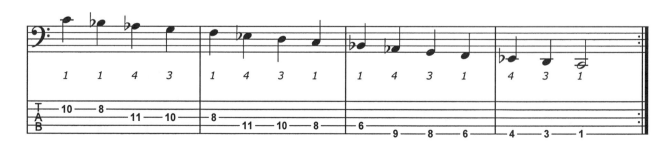

D Minor

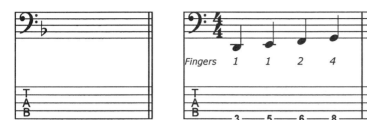

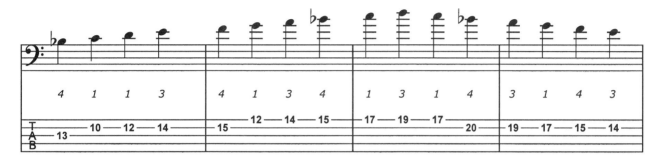

E Minor

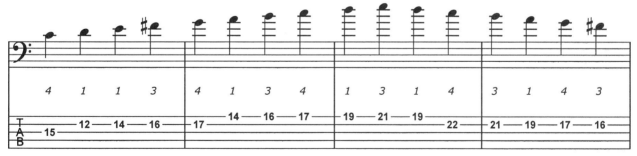

The Locrian Mode

Major scale

Locrian mode

C Locrian (construction)

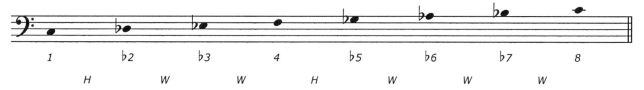

1	♭2	♭3	4	♭5	♭6	♭7	8
H	W	W	H	W	W	W

One octave scale

Chords

C°   Cm^{7(♭5)}

$Cm^{7(♭5)}$

2 Octaves

C Locrian

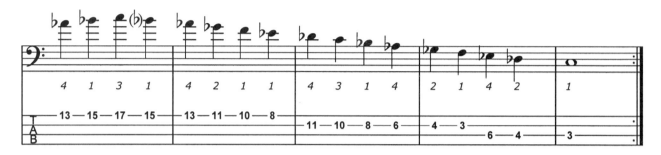

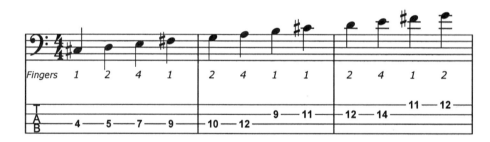

C♯ Locrian

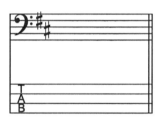

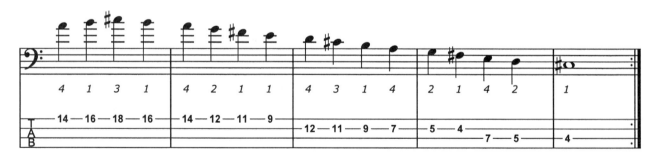

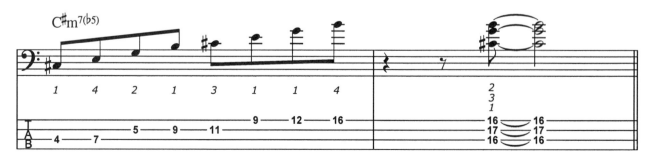

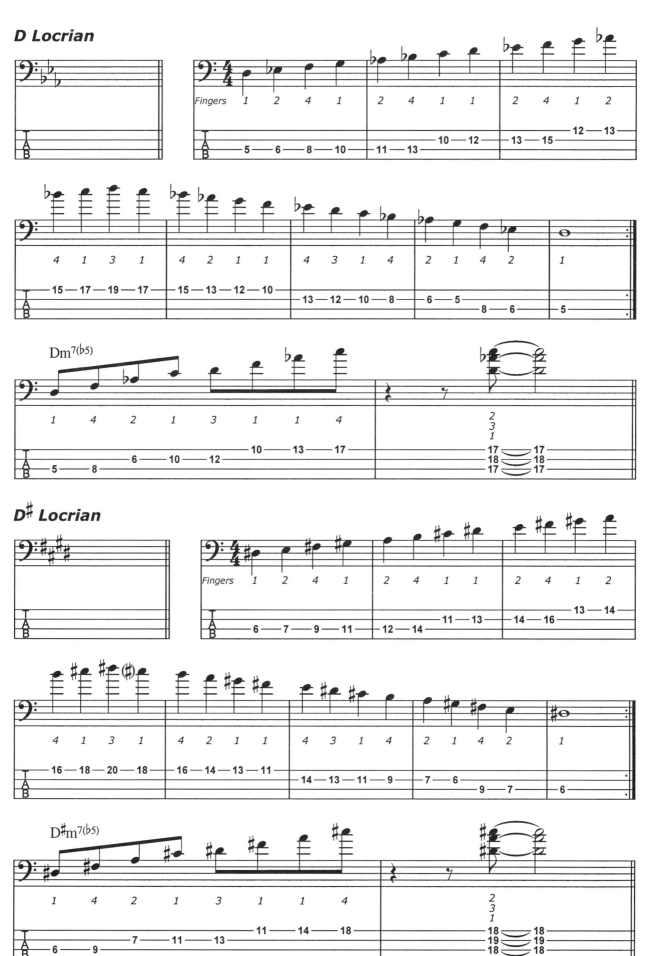

2 Octaves

E Locrian

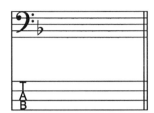

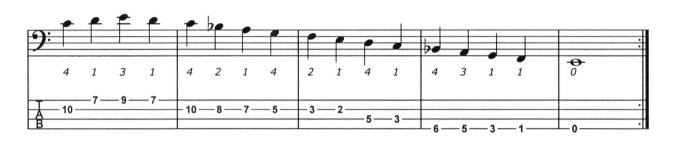

Em⁷⁽♭⁵⁾

F Locrian

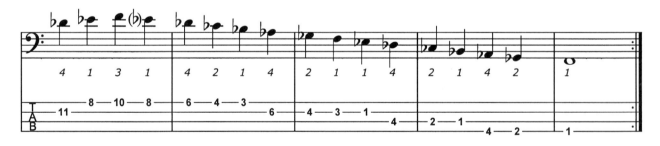

Fm⁷⁽♭⁵⁾

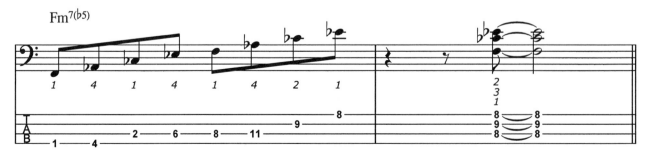

68

F# Locrian

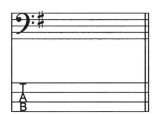

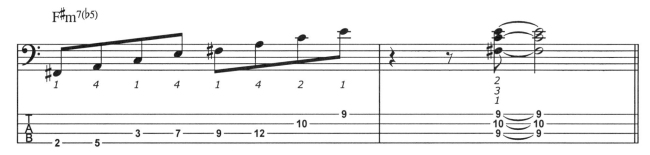

G Locrian

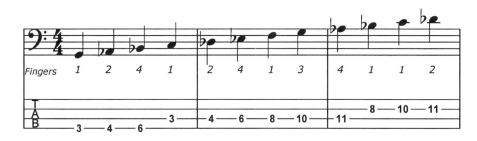

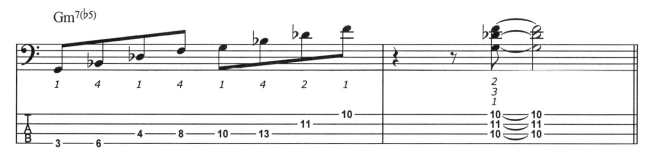

2 Octaves

G# Locrian

A Locrian

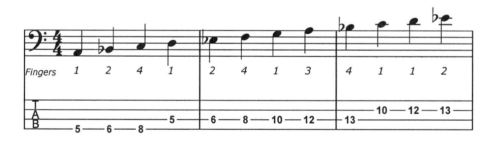

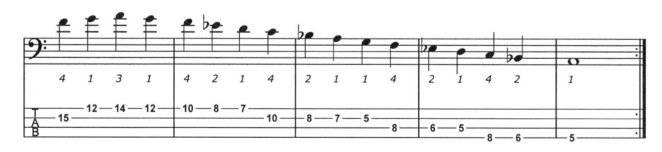

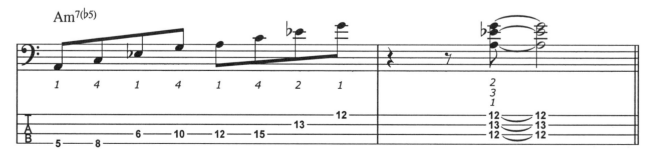

Locrian Mode

A# Locrian

B Locrian

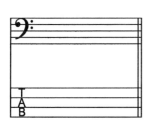

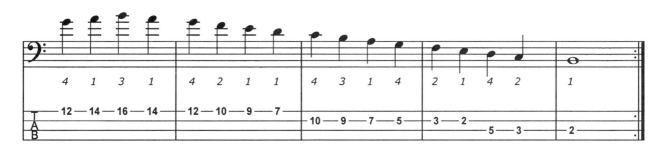

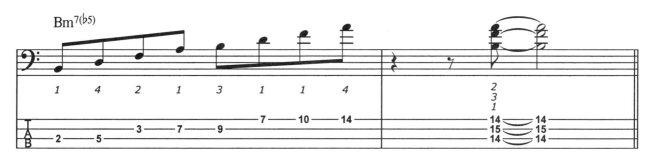

3 Octaves

B Locrian

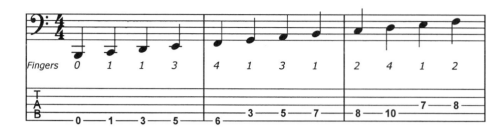

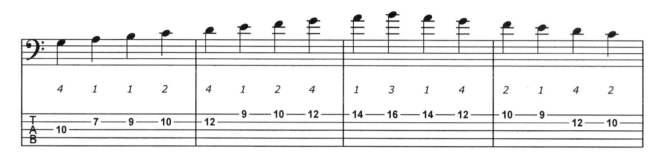

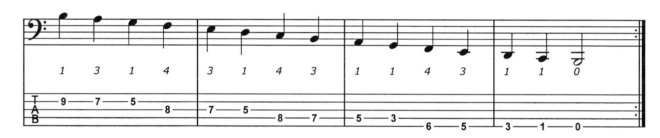

C Locrian

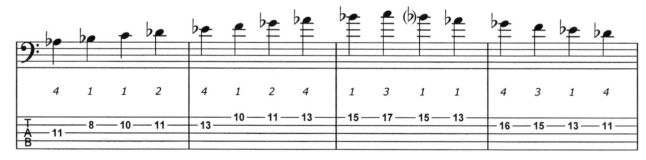

D Locrian

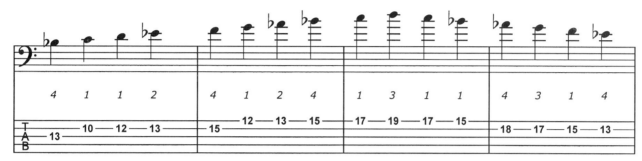

E Locrian

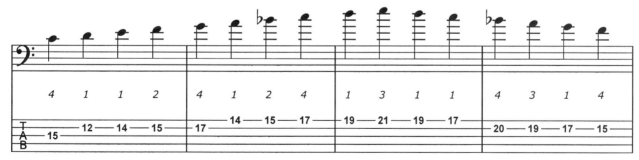

The PENTATONIC Family

The Major Pentatonic Scale

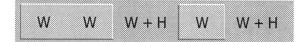

Major Pentatonic scale (Major Pentatonic - Mode 1)

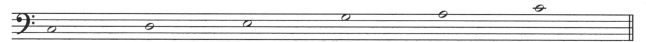

C Major Pentatonic (construction)

One octave scale

Chords

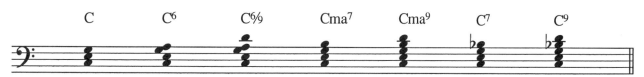

2 Octaves

C Major Pentatonic (Mode 1)

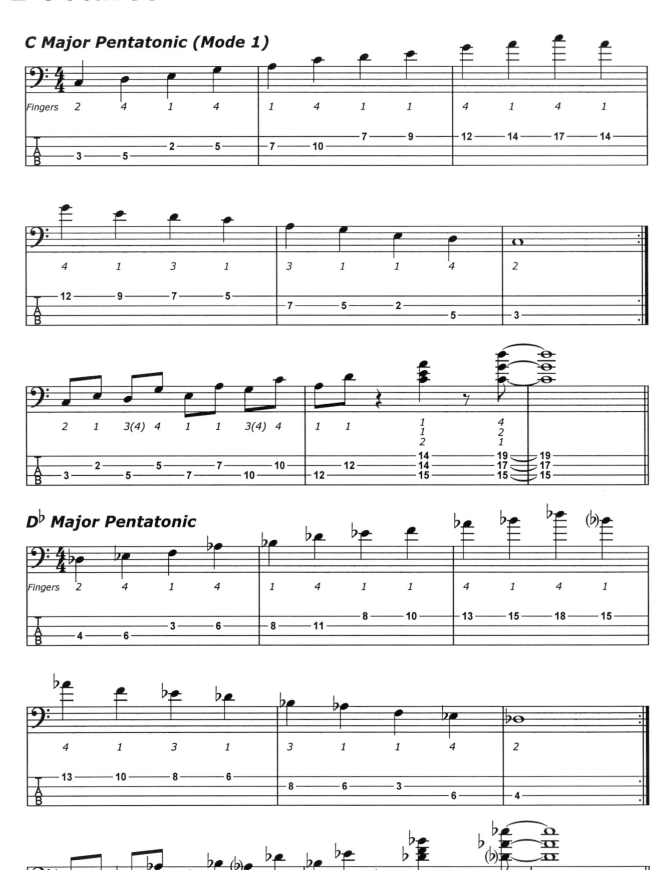

D♭ Major Pentatonic

Major Pentatonic Scale

D Major Pentatonic

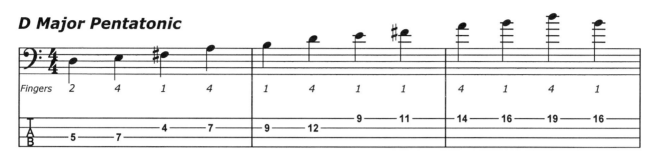

E♭ Major Pentatonic

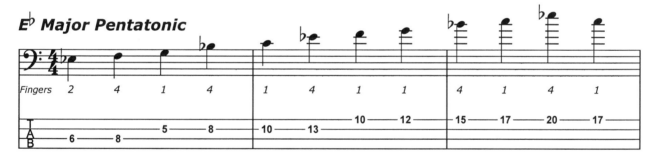

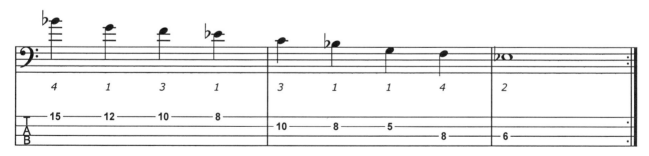

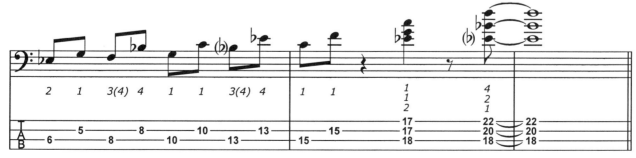

2 Octaves

E Major Pentatonic

F Major Pentatonic

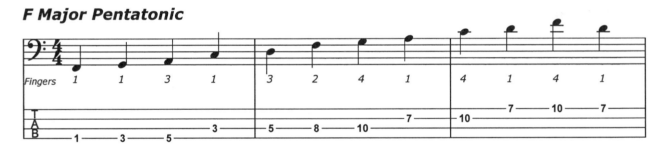

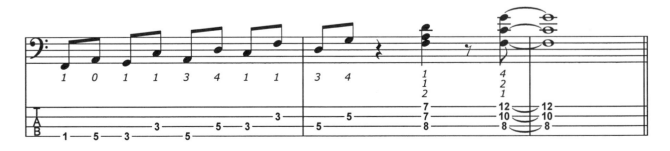

F# Major Pentatonic

G Major Pentatonic

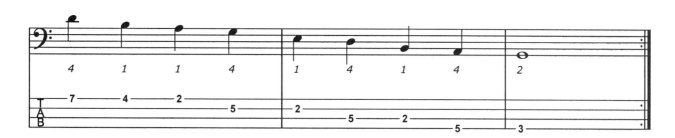

2 Octaves

A♭ Major Pentatonic

A Major Pentatonic

B♭ Major Pentatonic

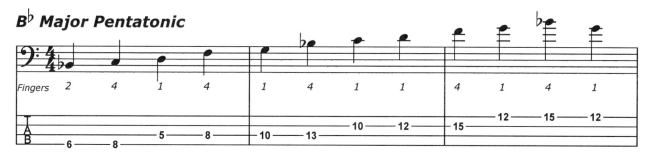

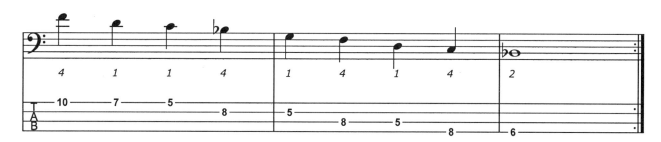

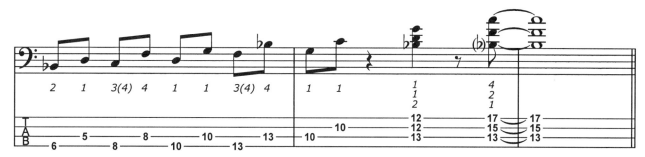

B Major Pentatonic

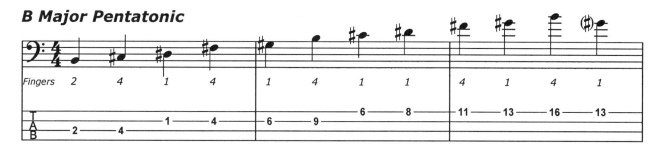

3 Octaves

B Major Pentatonic

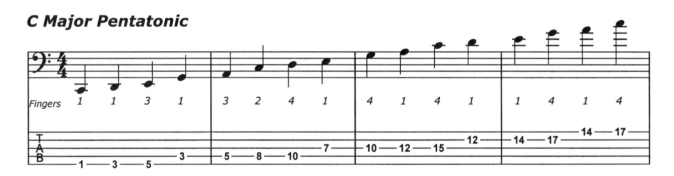

C Major Pentatonic

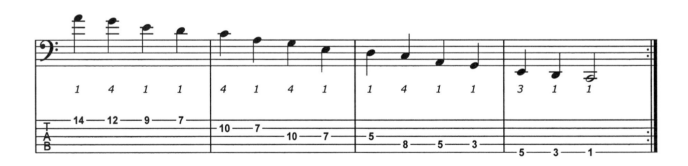

Major Pentatonic Scale

D Major Pentatonic

E Major Pentatonic

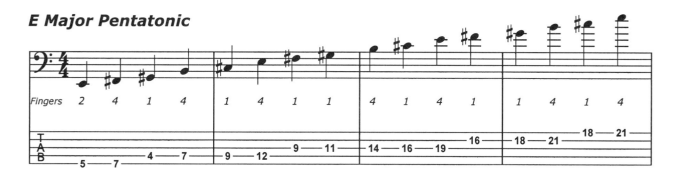

The Major Pentatonic - Mode 2

Major Pentatonic scale

Major Pentatonic - Mode 2

C Pentatonic - Mode 2 (construction)

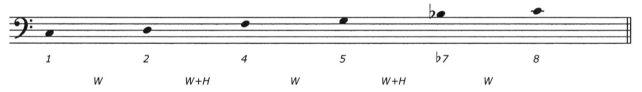

One octave scale

Chords

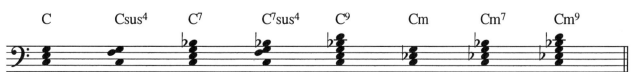

2 Octaves

C Pentatonic - Mode 2

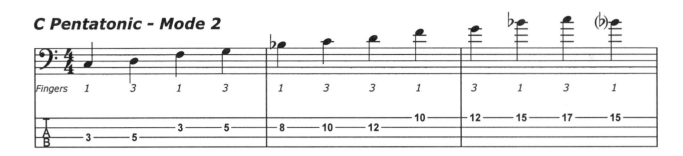

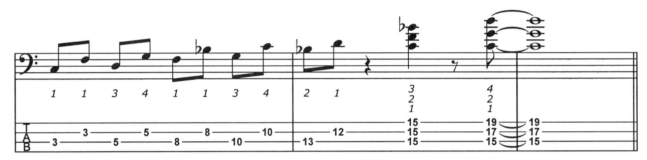

C# Pentatonic - Mode 2

86

D Pentatonic - Mode 2

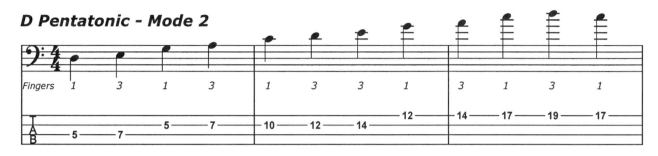

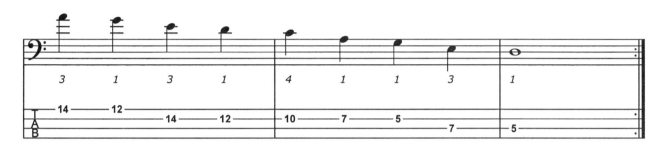

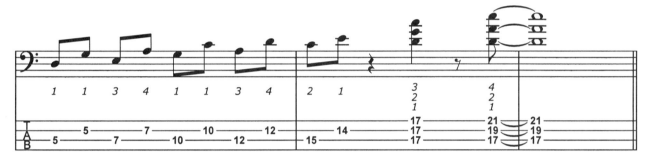

E♭ Pentatonic - Mode 2

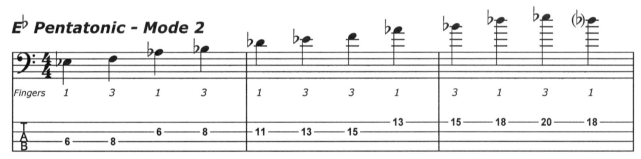

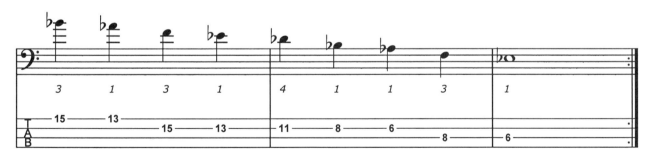

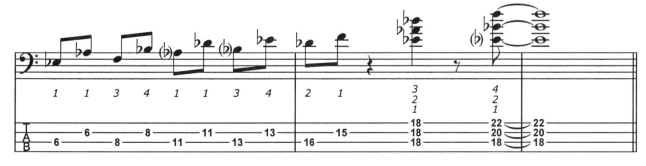

2 Octaves

E Pentatonic - Mode 2

F Pentatonic - Mode 2

F# Pentatonic - Mode 2

G Pentatonic - Mode 2

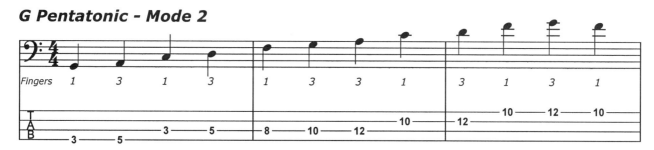

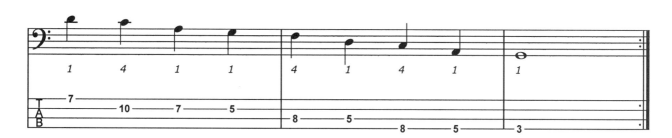

2 Octaves

A♭ Pentatonic - Mode 2

A Pentatonic - Mode 2

B♭ Pentatonic - Mode 2

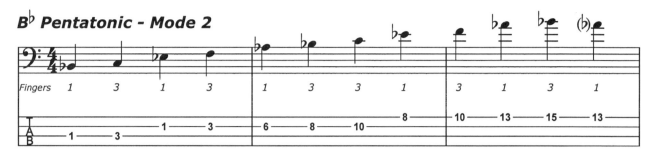

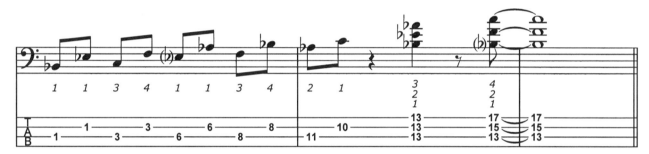

B Pentatonic - Mode 2

3 Octaves

B Pentatonic - Mode 2

C Pentatonic - Mode 2

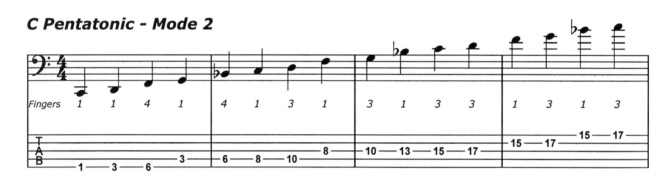

D Pentatonic - Mode 2

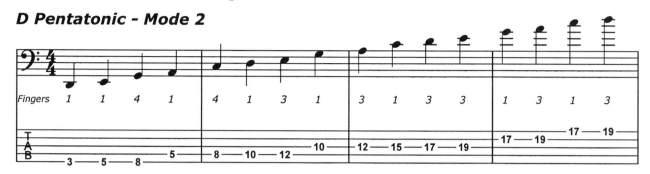

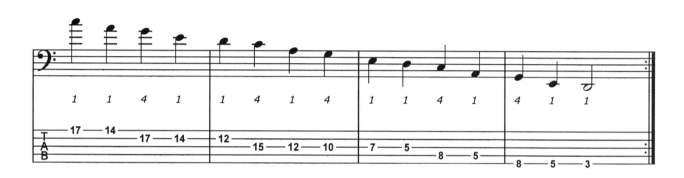

E Pentatonic - Mode 2

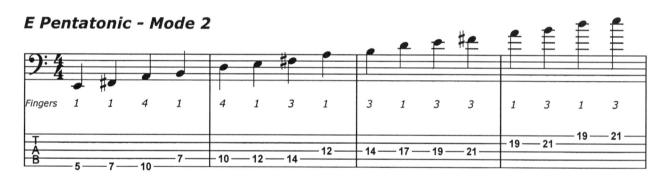

The Major Pentatonic - Mode 3

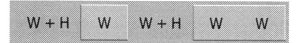

Major Pentatonic scale

Major Pentatonic - Mode 3

C Pentatonic - Mode 3 (construction)

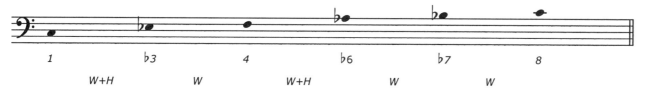

1	b3	4	b6	b7	8
W+H	W	W+H	W	W	

One octave scale

Chords

2 Octaves

C Pentatonic - Mode 3

C# Pentatonic - Mode 3

D Pentatonic - Mode 3

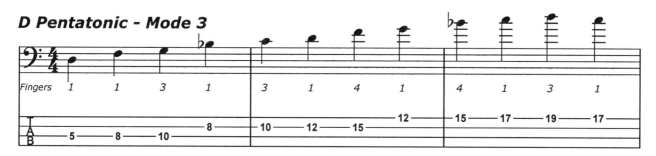

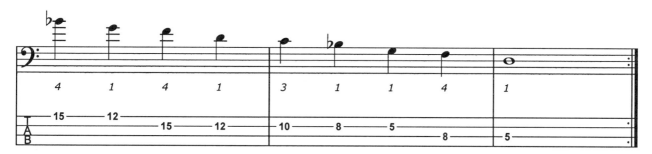

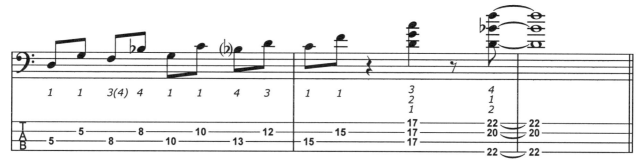

D# Pentatonic - Mode 3

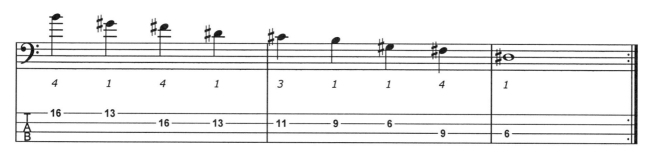

2 Octaves

E Pentatonic - Mode 3

F Pentatonic - Mode 3

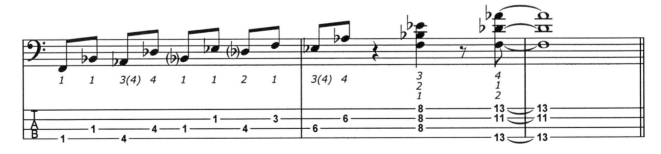

F# Pentatonic - Mode 3

G Pentatonic - Mode 3

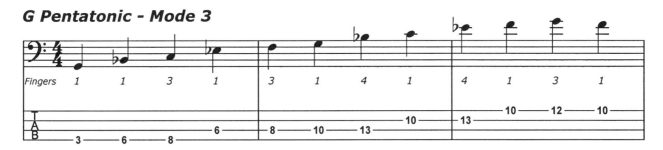

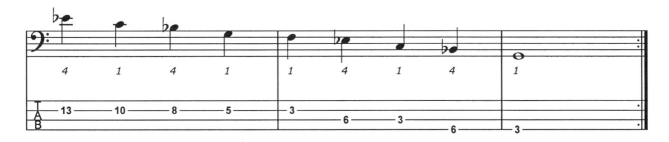

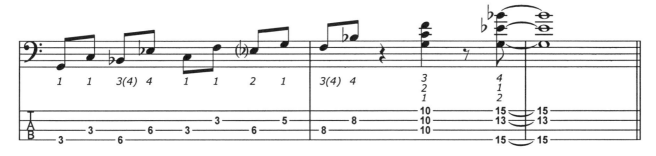

2 Octaves

G# Pentatonic - Mode 3

A Pentatonic - Mode 3

B♭ Pentatonic - Mode 3

B Pentatonic - Mode 3

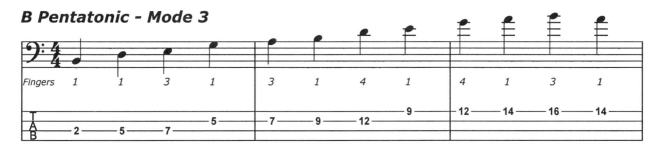

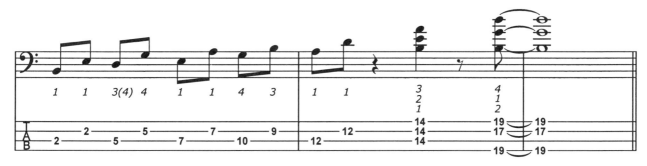

3 Octaves

B Pentatonic - Mode 3

C Pentatonic - Mode 3

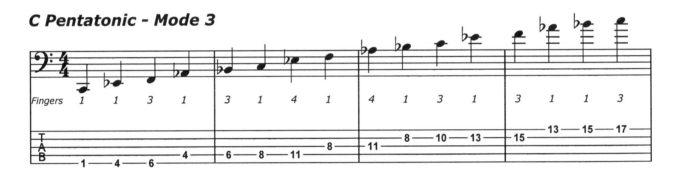

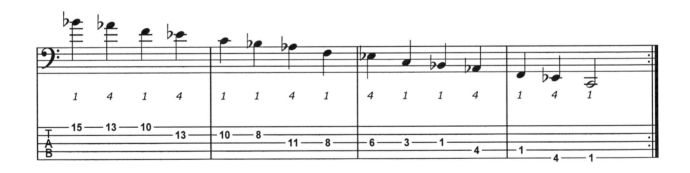

102

D Pentatonic - Mode 3

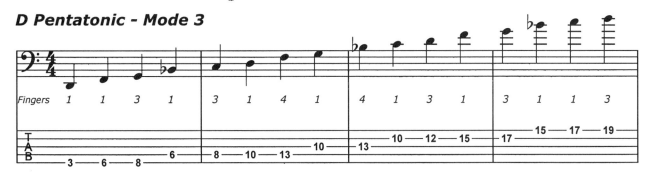

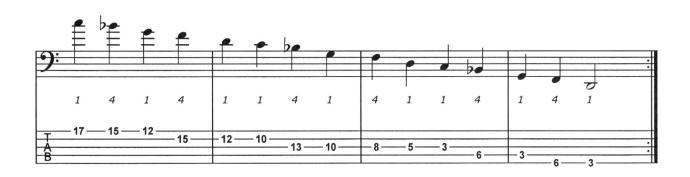

E Pentatonic - Mode 3

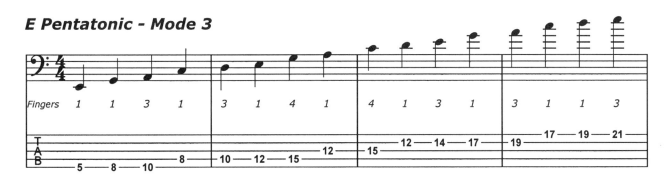

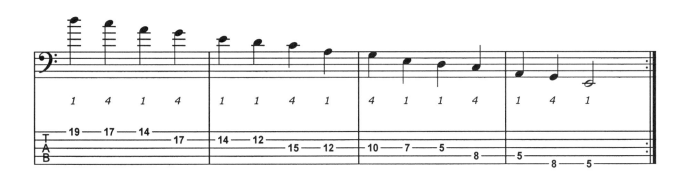

The Major Pentatonic - Mode 4

Major Pentatonic scale

C Pentatonic - Mode 4 (construction)

Major Pentatonic - Mode 4

One octave scale

Chords

2 Octaves

C Pentatonic - Mode 4

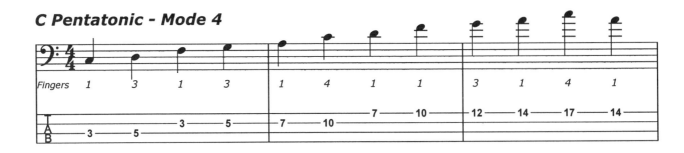

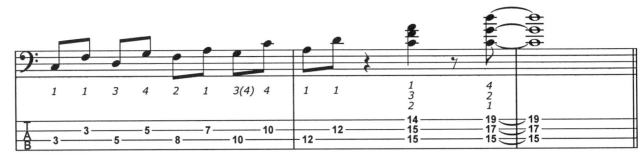

Db Pentatonic - Mode 4

D Pentatonic - Mode 4

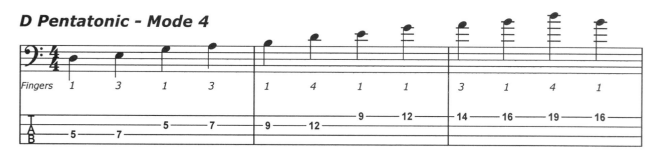

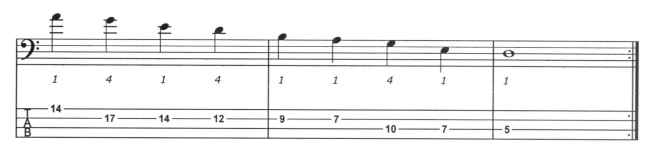

E♭ Pentatonic - Mode 4

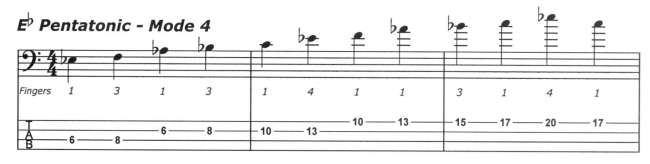

2 Octaves

E Pentatonic - Mode 4

F Pentatonic - Mode 4

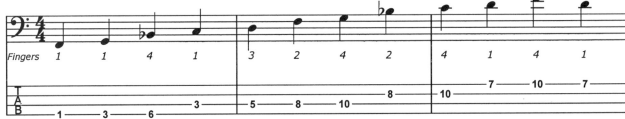

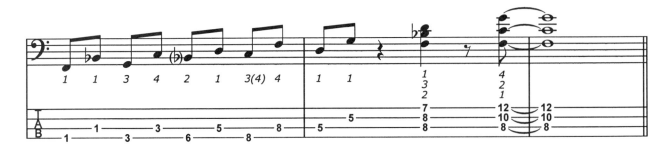

Major Pentatonic - Mode 4

F# Pentatonic - Mode 4

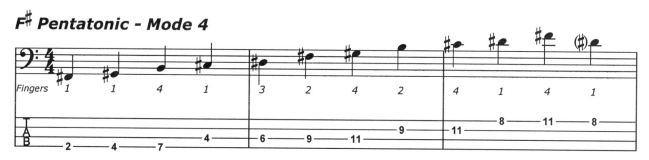

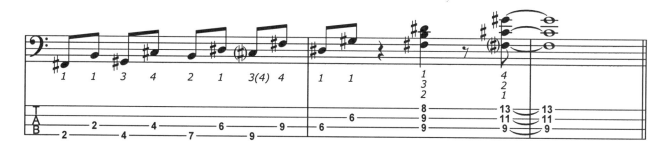

G Pentatonic - Mode 4

2 Octaves

A♭ Pentatonic - Mode 4

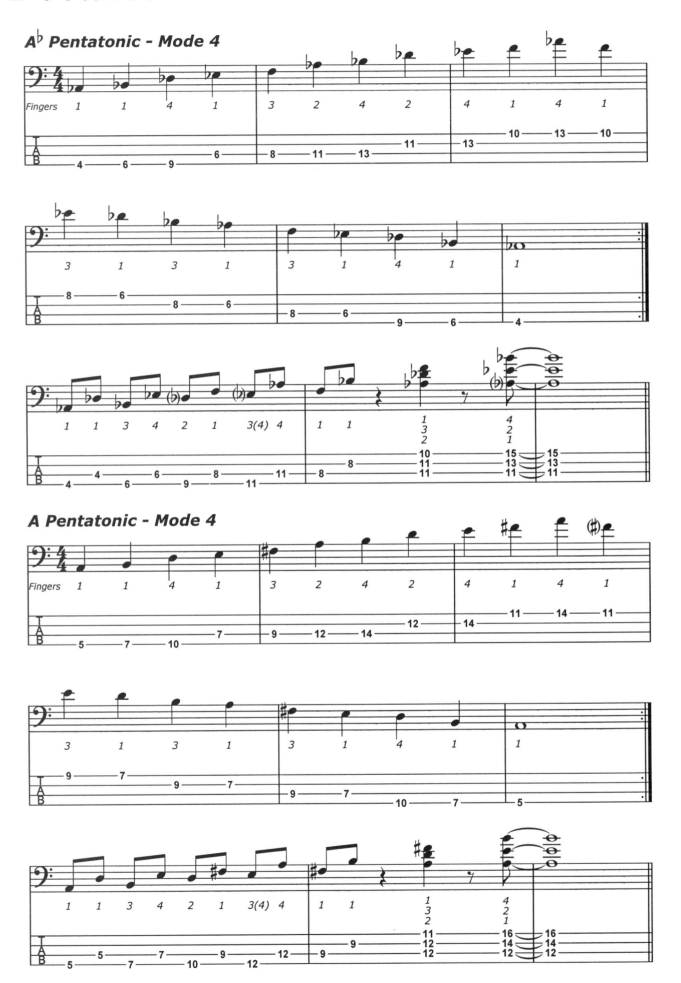

A Pentatonic - Mode 4

Major Pentatonic - Mode 4

B♭ Pentatonic - Mode 4

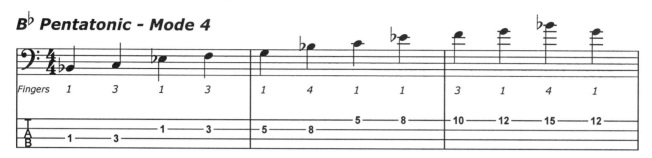

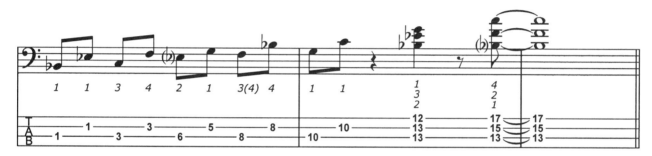

B Pentatonic - Mode 4

3 Octaves

B Pentatonic - Mode 4

C Pentatonic - Mode 4

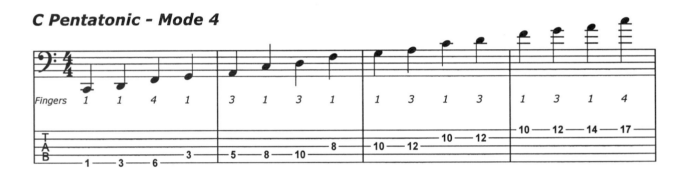

Major Pentatonic - Mode 4

D Pentatonic - Mode 4

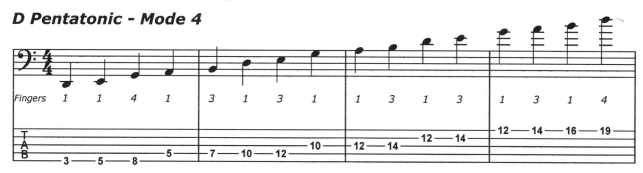

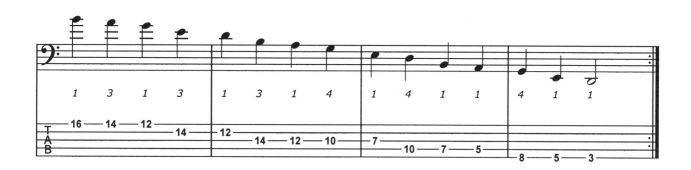

E Pentatonic - Mode 4

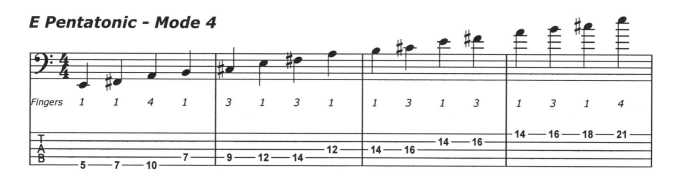

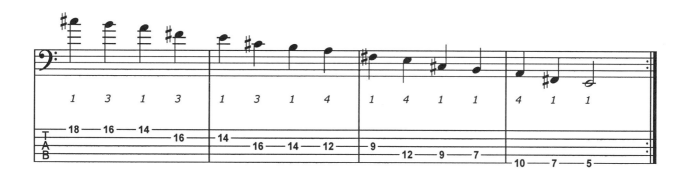

The Minor Pentatonic Scale

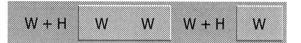

Major Pentatonic scale

**Minor Pentatonic scale
(Major Pentatonic - Mode 5)**

C Minor Pentatonic (construction)

One octave scale

Chords

2 Octaves

C Minor Pentatonic (Major Pentatonic - Mode 5)

C# Minor Pentatonic

D Minor Pentatonic

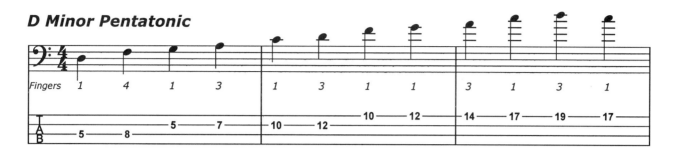

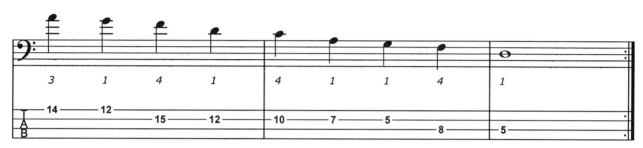

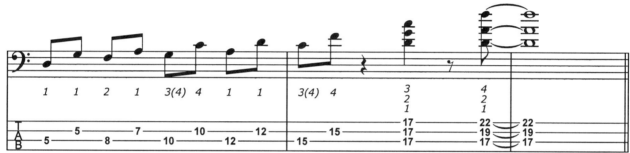

E♭ Minor Pentatonic

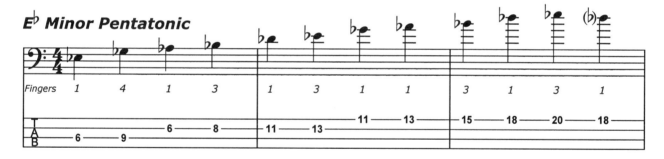

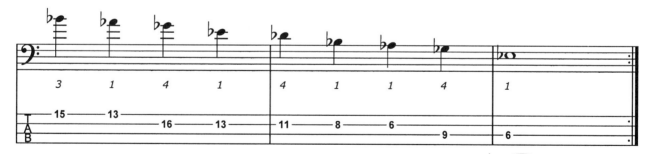

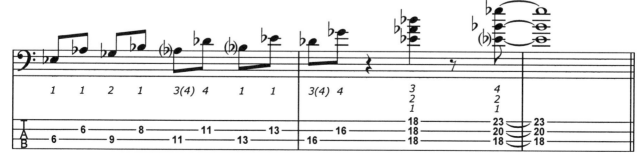

2 Octaves

E Minor Pentatonic

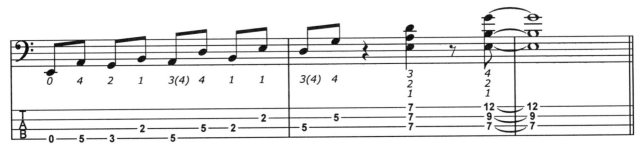

F Minor Pentatonic

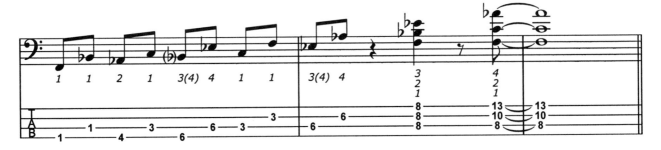

Minor Pentatonic Scale

F# Minor Pentatonic

G Minor Pentatonic

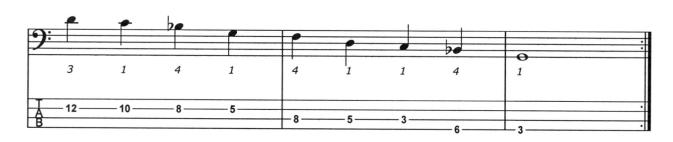

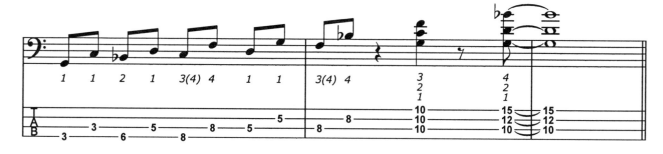

2 Octaves

G# Minor Pentatonic

A Minor Pentatonic

B♭ Minor Pentatonic

B Minor Pentatonic

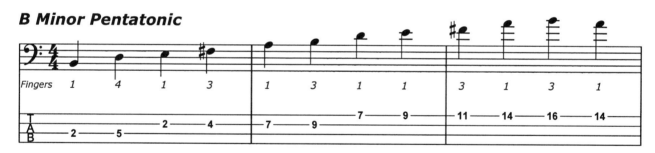

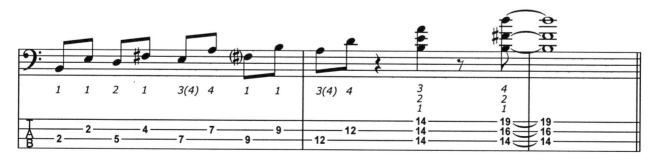

3 Octaves

B Minor Pentatonic

C Minor Pentatonic

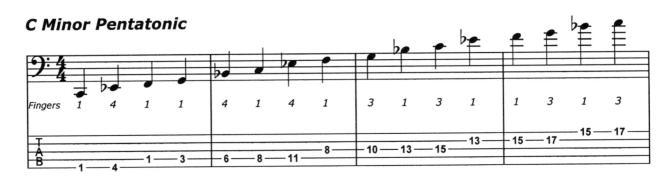

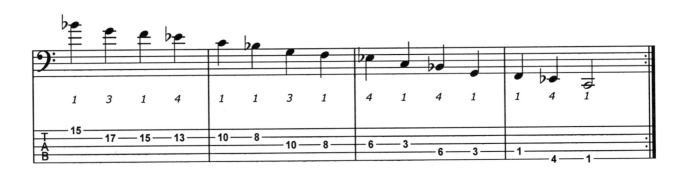

D Minor Pentatonic

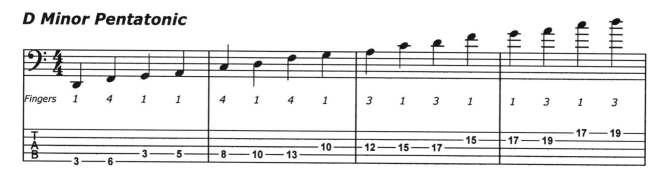

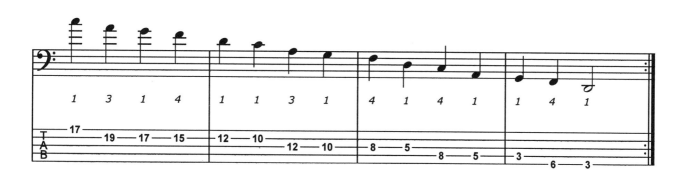

E Minor Pentatonic

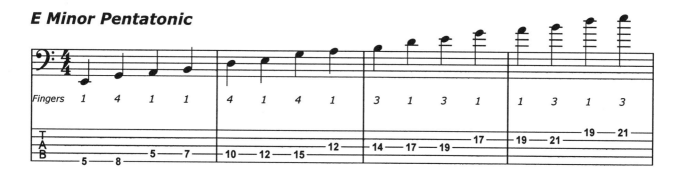

The *Just Jazz Real Book* features 250 classic jazz tunes. These songs form the required core repertoire for all working jazz musicians.